DOMINOES

Sherlock Holmes: The Norwood Mystery

LEVEL 2   700 HEADWORDS

OXFORD
UNIVERSITY PRESS

Great Clarendon Street, Oxford OX2 6DP

Oxford University Press is a department of the University of Oxford.
It furthers the University's objective of excellence in research, scholarship,
and education by publishing worldwide in

Oxford New York

Auckland Cape Town Dar es Salaam Hong Kong Karachi
Kuala Lumpur Madrid Melbourne Mexico City Nairobi
New Delhi Shanghai Taipei Toronto

With offices in

Argentina Austria Brazil Chile Czech Republic France Greece
Guatemala Hungary Italy Japan Poland Portugal Singapore
South Korea Switzerland Thailand Turkey Ukraine Vietnam

OXFORD and OXFORD ENGLISH are registered trade marks of
Oxford University Press in the UK and in certain other countries

ISBN: 978 0 19 424883 9 BOOK
ISBN: 978 0 19 463964 4 BOOK AND AUDIO PACK

No unauthorized photocopying

ACKNOWLEDGEMENTS

Illustrations by: Susan Scott

The publisher would like to thank the following for permission to reproduce photographs: Corbis pp 58
(Sir Arthur Conan Doyle/Hulton-Deutsch Collection), 59 (Alexander McCall Smith/Colin
Mcpherson); Getty Images pp 60 (Agatha Christie/Hulton Archive), 60 (Raymond Chandler/
Time & Life Pictures). pp 60 Angus Muir/Barbara Nadel, Michael Trevillion/Lindsey Davies
(both photos from authors agents).

DOMINOES

Series Editors: Bill Bowler and Sue Parminter

Sherlock Holmes: The Norwood Mystery

Sir Arthur Conan Doyle

Text adaptation by Jeremy Page

Illustrated by Susan Scott

Sir Arthur Conan Doyle (1859–1930), born in Edinburgh, Scotland, is best known as the creator of Sherlock Holmes. He started writing after working as a doctor and soon became one of the world's best-known authors. Four other books by Conan Doyle are also available as Dominoes: three Sherlock Holmes stories, *The Blue Diamond*, *The Emerald Crown* and *The Sign of Four*, and an adventure story, *The Lost World*.

OXFORD
UNIVERSITY PRESS

BEFORE READING

1 Write sentences describing these people from *The Norwood Mystery*.

a Sherlock Holmes

b Doctor Watson

c John McFarlane

d Inspector Lestrade

e Mrs McFarlane

f Sergeant Judd

g Mrs Lexington

h Jonas Oldacre

2 Which of these things do you think you will read about? Tick two boxes.

a ☐ Sherlock Holmes tries to find the murderer of Mrs McFarlane.

b ☐ Jonas Oldacre marries Mrs McFarlane.

c ☐ Inspector Lestrade arrests John McFarlane for murder.

d ☐ Mrs Lexington asks Sherlock Holmes for help.

e ☐ Sherlock Holmes saves an innocent man.

f ☐ Sergeant Judd is a criminal.

g ☐ Dr Watson investigates a murder without Holmes.

Chapter one

A wild, excited young man

'Life in London is not what it was,' said Sherlock Holmes to Dr Watson. They were sitting at the breakfast table in their Baker Street rooms one morning in the summer of 1894. Holmes was smoking a cigarette and Watson was reading the newspaper.

'True, Holmes,' said the doctor. 'For most people life is much better now.'

'But for me, Watson, life is not so interesting,' explained Holmes. 'I loved to read the newspaper, hoping to find some news of an interesting crime for me to **investigate** or a dangerous **criminal** for me to catch. Where are all those clever criminals these days?' He smiled **sadly**.

'Sometimes I don't understand you, Holmes,' said Watson. 'I like living a quiet life myself.'

Holmes did not reply, but opened his newspaper in a lazy way and started to read. Suddenly they heard a loud **knock** at the street door downstairs. They heard the knock again

investigate to find out about something

criminal a person who does something that is against the law

sadly in an unhappy way

knock the noise when someone hits a door

and again. Mrs Hudson, the **housekeeper**, ran to open the door and a wild, excited young man fell into the **hall**. He pushed the poor housekeeper out of his way and ran up the stairs.

'Who are you, sir?' asked Watson. 'And what do you want?'

The young man looked at Watson, then at Holmes, and started to explain.

'I'm sorry, Mr Holmes, I'm sorry,' he said. 'Please don't be angry. I feel so afraid, Mr Holmes.'

Holmes asked the young man to come into the room and told him to sit down.

'Have a cigarette,' he said, 'and tell us who you are and why you have come here.'

The man took a cigarette from the box on the table, and Watson lit it for him. After some minutes he stopped shaking and spoke.

'My name is John McFarlane,' he began. Neither Holmes nor Watson knew the name.

'And?' asked Holmes.

'And,' replied McFarlane, starting to shake again, 'I am in terrible **trouble**. You must help me, Mr Holmes. The police want to **arrest** me and send me to prison. And I have done nothing, Mr Holmes, nothing.'

'Interesting,' said Holmes, 'very interesting. Don't you agree, Watson?'

Watson saw that his friend was excited by this **mystery**, and wanted to know more.

'Mr McFarlane,' Holmes went on, 'why do the police want to arrest you? What have you done?'

'Nothing. I told you, I've done nothing. But they think that I murdered a man called Jonas Oldacre, a **builder** who lives – who lived – in south London, at Norwood.'

Holmes lit another cigarette. 'I'm very sorry to hear this, Mr McFarlane. Please tell us your story.'

housekeeper a woman who looks after a person's house

hall a room in the middle of a house from which you can go to all the other rooms

trouble difficulty

arrest to take a person to prison

mystery something that you cannot explain easily

builder a man who makes houses

2

McFarlane saw Watson's newspaper on the breakfast table and opened it.

'It's here,' he said, 'in today's newspaper. The story of the murder of Jonas Oldacre. I'll read it to you. *Terrible crime at Norwood. Murder of well-known builder.* The police are sure that I am the man who killed him. They've followed me here from the station and are waiting to arrest me. This news will kill my poor old mother, Mr Holmes, it will kill her.'

McFarlane was still shaking and smoking his cigarette. Watson looked at him in an interested way. McFarlane was a good-looking young man with bright blue eyes and long hair, but he looked very afraid. He was about twenty-seven years old and Watson could see that he came from a good family.

'If the police are following you,' said Holmes, 'we must work quickly. Mr McFarlane, please have another cigarette.

Watson, could you take the newspaper and read us the story?'

Watson opened the newspaper and started to read.

Sherlock Holmes listened carefully, his eyes closed, as Watson read the story from the morning newspaper.

Murder of well-known builder

Late last night, or early this morning, a terrible crime took place at Norwood in south London. Mr Jonas Oldacre has lived at Norwood and has worked there as a builder for many years. He is fifty-two years old, unmarried, and he lives in Deep Dene House on the Sydenham Road. The people of Norwood know Mr Oldacre as an unusual man. He does not often leave his house, but his business has made him very rich. There is a small **timber yard** behind his house and last night, at about midnight, a man who was out walking saw that some of the wood there was on fire. He immediately called the **fire brigade**, who arrived soon after. The wood was very dry and burned quickly, so it was impossible to **put out** the fire. The fire brigade were surprised when Mr Oldacre did not come out of the house, and two of their officers went inside to look for him. But Mr Oldacre was not in the house. In the bedroom the two men found an open **safe**, which was empty. There were papers on the floor and **bloodstains** on the walls. The men also found a bloodstained **walking stick** in the room. This stick belongs to Mr John McFarlane, who visited Mr Oldacre at his home yesterday evening. The police are sure that they know the **motive** for the crime and are looking for Mr McFarlane. They will arrest him when they find him. At Norwood, police now say that Mr Oldacre's bedroom windows on the ground floor of the house were open. They have found some burnt **remains**, possibly of a body, in the fire in the timber yard. The police think that there has been a murder. They say that the criminal killed the builder in his bedroom, then pulled his dead body into the garden and burned it in the timber yard. Inspector Lestrade of Scotland Yard is the policeman who is investigating this most terrible crime.

timber yard a place where wood is kept

fire brigade if your house is on fire, you call the fire brigade

put out to stop something burning

safe a very strong box that people put money and other expensive things in

bloodstains marks made by blood

walking stick a stick to help you walk

motive the reason for a crime

remains what is left

'This is very interesting,' he said at last. 'Can I ask, Mr McFarlane, why the police have not already arrested you? I understand from the newspaper that they are sure you murdered Mr Oldacre.'

'I live at Torrington Lodge, Blackheath, with my mother and father, Mr Holmes, but last night, after my business with Mr Oldacre, I stayed in a hotel at Norwood and went to work from there this morning. I knew nothing about this crime until I was on the train, when I read the story in the newspaper. I understood immediately that I was in terrible trouble, so when my train arrived at the station I ran to Baker Street to see you, Mr Holmes, and to tell you that I am not a criminal. I did not murder Mr Jonas Oldacre. The police, I'm sure, were waiting for me at work and also at my father's house at Blackheath. A man followed me here from the station and—'

Suddenly there was another knock at the street door. Then they heard men on the stairs, and Inspector Lestrade entered the room with two other policemen.

'Are you Mr John McFarlane?' he asked.

The young man stood up, his face white.

'I am,' he said.

Lestrade gave him a long look. 'John McFarlane, I am arresting you for the murder of Mr Jonas Oldacre, the builder, of Norwood, south London.'

READING CHECK

1 Are these sentences true or false? Tick the boxes.

		True	False
a	Holmes and Watson are sitting at the breakfast table when John McFarlane knocks on their door.	☑	☐
b	Holmes's housekeeper, Mrs Hudson, opens the door to McFarlane.	☐	☐
c	McFarlane is very excited.	☐	☐
d	Watson knows McFarlane's name.	☐	☐
e	McFarlane says that the police want to send him to prison.	☐	☐
f	Jonas Oldacre lives in Blackheath.	☐	☐
g	McFarlane lives alone.	☐	☐
h	Lestrade wants to arrest McFarlane for the murder of Jonas Oldacre.	☐	☐

2 Match the first and second parts of the sentences.

a 'Where are all those clever criminals?' ——— **1** says Lestrade to McFarlane.

b 'I like living a quiet life myself,' ——— **2** Holmes asks Watson.

c 'The police want to arrest me,' **3** says Watson to Holmes.

d 'He comes from a good family,' **4** Holmes asks McFarlane.

e 'Can I ask why the police have not already arrested you?' **5** says McFarlane to Holmes.

f 'I am arresting you for the murder of Jonas Oldacre,' **6** thinks Watson about McFarlane.

ACTIVITIES

WORD WORK

1 Correct the boxed words in these sentences. They all come from Chapter 1.

a There were important papers in the sale . . . . . *safe* . . . .

b A young man came into the ball . . . .

c They heard a clock at the door. . . . .

d He had a talking brick in his hand. . . . .

e What was his motor for killing the man? . . . .

f He explained that he was in terrible tremble . . . .

g Holmes was excited by the history . . . .

h Jonas Oldacre was a south London building . . . .

i There were floodstains on the walls. . . . .

j The police found some burnt reminds in the timber-yard. . . . .

k Can you put off that fire with some water? . . . .

l She cried badly when her cat died. . . . .

GUESS WHAT

What happens in the next chapter? Tick four boxes.

a ☐ Holmes listens to McFarlane's story.

b ☐ We learn more about Inspector Lestrade.

c ☐ We learn more about McFarlane's family.

d ☐ Lestrade asks McFarlane some questions.

e ☐ McFarlane says that he killed Jonas Oldacre.

f ☐ Holmes decides to go to Blackheath.

g ☐ The police take McFarlane away.

h ☐ Lestrade has breakfast with Holmes and Watson.

Chapter two

McFarlane's story

McFarlane put his head in his hands and sat down. 'Mr Holmes, help me, please.'

Holmes turned to Lestrade. 'Inspector,' he said, 'perhaps you can give us half an hour? I'm interested to hear Mr McFarlane's story.'

'And I'm sure it will be a very good story,' replied Lestrade. 'But it won't be true.'

'Please, Inspector,' said Watson.

Lestrade thought for a long time. 'All right,' he agreed at last. 'You've often helped us, Mr Holmes. But I must stay with Mr McFarlane and I will listen very carefully to everything that he says. You have half an hour,' he went on, looking at his watch.

'Thank you, Inspector,' said McFarlane.

'You can thank Mr Holmes,' replied Lestrade, sitting down opposite the young man.

'First,' McFarlane began his story, 'I know nothing about Mr Jonas Oldacre, only his name. My parents met him many years ago and they were friends for a long time. But Mr Oldacre moved to Norwood, I understand, and after that they never saw him. So I was very surprised when he walked into my office at three o'clock yesterday afternoon. I work in **the City** of London as a **lawyer**. When he told me why he wanted to see me, I was **astonished**.' Here he stopped and looked first at Holmes, then at Lestrade.

'Go on,' said Lestrade at last.

'He had some papers in his hand, these papers.' McFarlane took them out of his pocket and put them on the table. '"This is my **will**," he said. "I've written it myself. But you are a lawyer. Please **copy** it for me. I will wait." I agreed to do this. I started to copy the will but was very surprised

the City a part of London with a lot of banks and offices

lawyer someone who works to help people with the law

astonished very surprised

will the paper that you write and sign, which says how you want to divide your money between people in your family when you die

copy to write something again

when I read that he wanted to leave everything to me! Mr Oldacre was a strange little man with very white hair and grey eyes. When I looked at him, I saw that he found my surprise very funny. He laughed and told me that he was unmarried and had no children. He knew my mother and father when he was a young man and wanted to help me to make my way in the world because I was their son. I didn't know what to say, but I thanked him warmly and finished the will. Here it is.' McFarlane showed Holmes a blue piece of paper. 'Mr Oldacre then asked me to go to his house at Norwood yesterday evening because he had more papers there that I needed to see. I didn't want to go, but I had to. "You must promise not to tell your mother or father about this," he said. "It must be a wonderful surprise for them." I promised him that I would say nothing, but I didn't understand why it was so important to him.'

'I took the train to Norwood and arrived there at about nine o'clock. It was difficult to find Mr Oldacre's house on the Sydenham Road and it was nine-thirty when I at last knocked on the door of Deep Dene House.'

'Stop,' said Holmes. 'Who opened the door to you?'

'It was Mr Oldacre's housekeeper,' McFarlane replied. 'A woman of about fifty-five years.'

'And she told Mr Oldacre that you were there?' Holmes went on.

'That's right,' McFarlane agreed. 'She then took me into the **dining room**, where Mr Oldacre was waiting for me. We ate a light meal of sandwiches and fruit, then Mr Oldacre took me to his bedroom. There was a safe in the corner of the room, and Mr Oldacre opened it and took out a lot of papers. We looked at them together and didn't finish until about half past eleven. Mr Oldacre said that we mustn't wake up the housekeeper, so I left the house by the **French windows** in the bedroom, which were open. I couldn't find my walking stick, but Mr Oldacre said that he would give it back to me next time. "I hope you will come back often," he said. When I left, Mr Oldacre was in his bedroom and the safe was open. His papers were on the table. It was too late for me to go back to my father's house at Blackheath, so I went to a hotel called the Anerley Arms in Norwood and spent the night there. I knew nothing more about Mr Oldacre until I read the story in the newspaper this morning. And everything that I've told you is true.'

Lestrade looked at Holmes. 'Any more questions?'

'Possibly,' said Holmes. 'But first I must go to Blackheath.'

'You mean Norwood,' said Lestrade.

'Perhaps,' replied Holmes with a strange smile. The Inspector didn't understand, but said nothing.

'Mr McFarlane?' said one of the other policemen, who was waiting at the door. 'Come with us, please.'

dining room the room in a house where people eat

French windows glass doors

McFarlane stood up and the two policemen took him down the stairs and out into Baker Street. Lestrade stayed in the room with Holmes and Watson. Holmes looked at McFarlane's papers, which were still on the table.

'Interesting,' he said. 'Mr Oldacre's writing is very easy to read in some places, but very difficult to read in others. And here it's impossible. Can you read this, Watson?'

Watson agreed that it was impossible to read.

'And why is that?' asked Holmes.

'I've no idea,' Watson replied.

'Is this important, Mr Holmes?' asked Lestrade.

'Possibly,' said Holmes. 'Mr Oldacre wrote his will on a train. We can read everything that he wrote when the train was at a station, but it's impossible to read what he wrote when the train was moving. Mr Oldacre spent the journey writing his will, so his train was an express, which stopped only once between Norwood and London Bridge.'

'Very interesting, Mr Holmes,' said Lestrade, 'but I have a murderer to see. I must go. Goodbye, Mr Holmes. Dr Watson.'

'Goodbye, Inspector,' said Holmes with a smile.

READING CHECK

Put these sentences in the correct order. Number them 1–11.

a ☐ Oldacre asks McFarlane to copy his will.

b ☐ Oldacre and McFarlane eat sandwiches.

c ☐ McFarlane takes the train to Norwood.

d ☐ Oldacre takes papers out of his safe.

e ☐ Oldacre's housekeeper opens the door of Deep Dene House to McFarlane.

f ☐ Oldacre tells McFarlane that he wants to leave him everything in his will.

g ☐ Oldacre walks into McFarlane's office.

h ☐ McFarlane arrives at Deep Dene House.

i ☐ McFarlane spends the night at a hotel in Norwood.

j ☐ McFarlane leaves Deep Dene House through the French windows.

k ☐ Oldacre tells McFarlane to say nothing to his parents.

WORD WORK

Use the words in the safe to complete the sentences.

a He worked in an office in ..the City.. of London.

b McFarlane was .... that Oldacre wanted to leave him his money.

c A .... helps people when they have problems with the police.

d My grandmother left me £1,000 in her ....

e He asked me to .... the words very carefully on a piece of paper.

f They ate their dinner in the ....

g Let's open the .... and walk out into the garden.

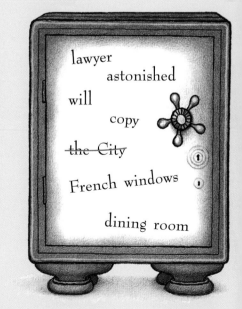

lawyer
astonished
will
copy
the City
French windows
dining room

12

GUESS WHAT

Who does Holmes speak to in the next chapter? Tick two pictures.

a ☐ Inspector Lestrade   **b** ☐ Dr Watson   **c** ☐ John McFarlane

d ☐ John McFarlane's mother   **e** ☐ John McFarlane's father

f ☐ Jonas Oldacre   **g** ☐ Jonas Oldacre's housekeeper

Chapter three

A visit to Blackheath

stupid not clever

'Tell me, Holmes,' said Watson when they were alone again, 'why is it important that Mr Oldacre wrote his will on the train?'

Holmes lit a cigarette. 'Because it means he wrote it yesterday on his journey to see Mr McFarlane. I think it's very strange that he worked on these important papers on the train. Perhaps they weren't so important for him.'

'What are you thinking, Holmes?' asked Watson.

'I'm not yet sure what has happened here, Watson,' Holmes replied, 'but give me time, give me time. Now I must leave you and go to Blackheath. I need, I think, to speak to Mr McFarlane's mother and father.'

Holmes put on his coat. 'While I am out, Watson, ask yourself this question. Is Mr McFarlane a **stupid** man? I think not. But does a clever man immediately kill someone who has just promised to leave him everything in his will?' Holmes gave Watson a long look. 'Goodbye, Watson. Until later.'

When Sherlock Holmes needed to think, he liked to walk, and this morning he decided to walk all the way from Baker Street to London Bridge. His long legs moved quickly as he crossed the city. A lot of people stopped to look at the tall detective as he made his way to the station, but Holmes didn't see them. He was thinking about John McFarlane and Jonas Oldacre, and asking himself if McFarlane was a murderer. He really didn't think so, but he knew that it would be difficult to **convince** Inspector Lestrade of Scotland Yard. To Lestrade, McFarlane was the murderer of Jonas Oldacre. He had a good motive and he spent the evening at the builder's house.

Holmes arrived at London Bridge station and found that he had to wait twenty minutes for the next train to Blackheath. He bought the late morning newspaper and read: *Norwood Murder. Man Arrested*. Holmes didn't read the story, but looked at the end: *Says Inspector Lestrade: 'I think we have our man.'* Holmes bought a ticket and got on the train. Soon he was leaving London and travelling south to Blackheath.

It was a little before eleven thirty when he knocked on the door of the McFarlanes' house. It was a large house with a long, green garden at the front, and Holmes was a little surprised when Mrs McFarlane herself answered the door.

'Mrs McFarlane? Good morning. My name is Sherlock Holmes and I am trying to help your son in his time of trouble.'

'Oh, Mr Holmes, please come in,' the woman replied.

Holmes followed her into a small room at the back of the house, where a fire was burning brightly. They sat down.

'John is not a murderer,' she began immediately. 'I know my son, Mr Holmes and—'

Holmes held up his hand.

convince to make someone believe something

'Mrs McFarlane,' he said, 'I can see that you're very worried, but there are some questions that I must ask you.'

'Anything,' she replied. 'Please ask me anything.'

'What can you tell me about Mr Jonas Oldacre?'

At this question Mrs McFarlane was suddenly very excited.

'He is – or was – a very bad man,' she said. 'A long time ago he and I were friends. He wanted to marry me, but I found out that he was a **cruel** man, a dangerous man. I told him that I didn't want to see him again and six months later I married my husband, John's father. He wasn't rich like Oldacre, but he was a good man – he is a good man, Mr Holmes, and a good father to John. We've always been a happy family. And now this!'

'What did Oldacre do when you sent him away?' Holmes went on.

'He was angry, very angry. He sent me this in the post.'

Mrs McFarlane got up and took a photograph from the desk in the corner of the room. It was a photograph of her as a young woman. There were black **lines** across her face, where many years before Oldacre once **slashed** the photograph with a knife, but Holmes could see that she was a very beautiful woman.

'It arrived the day that I married my husband.'

Holmes took the photograph from her and looked at it **thoughtfully**.

'A dangerous man,' he said.

'Oh yes,' Mrs McFarlane agreed, 'a very dangerous man.'

'It is strange, then,' Holmes went on, 'that in his will he left everything that he had to your son.'

'We don't want anything from that man, Mr Holmes. If he's dead, then I'm happy, but I know that it wasn't John who killed him.'

Holmes stood up. 'Mrs McFarlane, thank you. Is Mr McFarlane not at home?'

cruel unkind and liking to hurt people

line a long thin mark

slash to cut wildly and angrily

thoughtfully thinking carefully

16

Mrs McFarlane shook her head. 'He's taken the train to London to see if he can help John,' she explained.

'Then I won't stay any longer,' said Holmes. 'Try not to worry too much, my good woman. If your son is really **innocent**, I'm sure we can convince the police. Inspector Lestrade is sometimes a little slow but he is a good detective.'

'Thank you, Mr Holmes,' said Mrs McFarlane. 'I'm sure that you will do everything that you can to help John.'

'Mrs McFarlane, you can be sure of that,' Holmes replied with a warm smile.

Mrs McFarlane said goodbye to the great detective at her front door and watched him walk quickly away to the station.

innocent having done nothing wrong

READING CHECK

Match the first and second parts of these sentences.

a Holmes thinks

b Holmes goes to Blackheath

c Lestrade is sure

d Holmes is surprised

e Mrs McFarlane tells Holmes

f John McFarlane's father

g Holmes tells McFarlane

1 that McFarlane is the murderer of Jonas Oldacre.

2 that Oldacre wrote his will on the train to London.

3 to speak to John McFarlane's parents.

4 that Jonas Oldacre was her friend.

5 has taken the train to London to try to help John.

6 that Lestrade is a good but slow detective.

7 when Mrs McFarlane opens the door.

WORD WORK

Find words in the train on page 19 to complete the sentences.

a The idea of John McFarlane murdering someone who is going to leave him everything is ...*stupid*....

b Mrs McFarlane tells Holmes that her son is ....

c Mrs McFarlane says that Oldacre was a very .... man.

d Oldacre once .... a photograph of Mrs McFarlane with a knife.

e Holmes looks at the old photograph very ....

f There are long black .... across young Mrs McFarlane's beautiful face.

g Holmes is sure he can .... Lestrade that John McFarlane is not a murderer.

DIPUST

RUCEL

TLUGHULTYFOH

OVENCINC

SINEL

TENCONIN

SLESADH

GUESS WHAT

What does Holmes do in the next chapter? Tick one of the boxes.

a ☐ He goes to Scotland Yard to talk to Inspector Lestrade.

b ☐ He visits John McFarlane in prison.

c ☐ He travels to Norwood.

d ☐ He goes back to Baker Street to talk to Dr Watson.

Chapter four

A visit to Norwood

Holmes arrived in Norwood early that afternoon. He had no problem finding Deep Dene House on the Sydenham Road. The builder's house was large and modern, and had a big garden with a lot of very old trees. Next to the house Holmes saw the timber yard, where the police found the burnt remains after the fire. He walked into it and saw piles of wood everywhere and also some bags of **hay**. On the ground he saw some burnt remains and he **crouched down** to look at them. Were these the remains of Jonas Oldacre's body? It was impossible to say. Holmes stood up and went back into the garden.

As he stood there looking thoughtfully at the house, a policeman came out.

'Can I help you, sir?' he asked.

'I'm Sherlock Holmes,' said the detective. 'Perhaps you've heard my name.'

'Mr Holmes! Of course I know your name, sir,' replied the policeman in surprise. He was fat, perhaps fifty years old, with a round face and bright blue eyes. 'Sergeant Judd, Scotland Yard. I'm very pleased to meet you, sir.'

'And I'm pleased to meet you,' said Holmes. 'I'm helping Inspector Lestrade with his **investigation**. Have you found anything here?'

Judd looked very pleased. His blue eyes **shone**.

'Yes, sir, we have. You know about the burnt remains in the timber yard, I **suppose**?'

'I do,' Holmes agreed. 'I've seen them for myself.'

'Well, we've found some **buttons** in the **ashes** – and we think they're the buttons from Mr Oldacre's trousers. It's murder, Mr Holmes, we're sure of that.'

'Perhaps,' said Holmes. 'But I prefer to decide for myself. Is it

hay dry grass

crouch down to bend your knees so that your body is close to the ground

investigation something that a detective does to understand how or why a crime has happened

shine (*past* **shone**) the sun shines in the sky

suppose to think that something is true

button a small round thing on clothes

ashes the grey stuff that you see after something has burnt

all right if I look round the house and garden, Sergeant?'

'Please do, Mr Holmes, but I think that you'll find that we're right. There's been a murder and Inspector Lestrade has arrested the criminal. We can all sleep better in our beds now that McFarlane is under arrest.'

Judd went back into the house while Holmes stayed outside in the garden. There were very few flowers and the garden was very different from the McFarlanes' garden in Blackheath. Holmes crouched down to look at the **lawn**. It was a warm day and the lawn was very dry. He

lawn the grass in a garden

looked carefully for more than an hour but found nothing interesting in the garden. Next he decided to **search** the house. The front door was open and a policeman was standing inside.

'Good morning,' said Holmes as he walked into the house.

At the end of the hall he found Oldacre's bedroom. There were no police in the room and Holmes spent a long time looking at the walls. He saw the bloodstains, which were a deep red colour, and on the floor **footprints** made by Oldacre and McFarlane. But he found no one else's footprints. He looked at the papers from the safe and he also found the builder's bank books. He spent a long time looking at these and was interested to see that Oldacre wasn't as rich as everyone thought. To Holmes' surprise, he had very little money in the bank.

He then tried to find the **deeds** to the house, but they were not with the other papers. Holmes asked himself why. When he was sure that there was nothing more to see in the bedroom, he crossed the hall to the kitchen, where he found Oldacre's housekeeper, Mrs Lexington, at the table. She was a small, dark, silent woman with grey eyes and silver hair. She didn't look at the detective when he walked into the room and spoke to her.

'Good morning. My name's Sherlock Holmes and I'm helping Scotland Yard with their investigation,' he said. 'Mrs . . . ?'

'Lexington,' she replied without looking up. 'Mrs Lexington, housekeeper to Mr Jonas Oldacre.'

'I'm very pleased to meet you, Mrs Lexington,' Holmes went on, and sat down opposite her at the table. 'What can you tell me about yesterday evening?'

The housekeeper gave Holmes a long look.

'Nothing,' she replied. 'There's nothing that I can tell you, Mr Sherlock Holmes.'

'Really?' said Holmes. 'So you didn't answer the door to Mr McFarlane last night?'

'I did!' she shouted angrily. 'The murderer!'

'Ah!' said Holmes. 'So there is something that you can tell me?'

Mrs Lexington looked very cross.

'I opened the front door of this house to McFarlane at 9.30. I know now that I opened the door to a murderer!'

'And then?' Holmes asked.

'Then nothing,' she said at last. 'I was very tired and I went to bed an hour later at half past ten. My bedroom is at the other end of the house. I fell asleep immediately. I heard nothing and I saw nothing.'

'Did you sleep all night without waking up?' asked Holmes.

'The smell from the fire woke me up,' Mrs Lexington answered. 'I got out of bed and started to look for Mr Oldacre. I looked in every room of the house but I couldn't find him anywhere. He was dead, of course, I know that now. McFarlane killed him and burnt his body in the timber yard. And Mr Oldacre was such a good, kind man . . .'

'Please,' said Holmes, 'don't **upset yourself**. Tell me, did Mr Oldacre have any enemies?'

'Everyone has enemies,' replied Mrs Lexington. 'But Mr Oldacre lived a very quiet life here at Deep Dene House. No one in Norwood wanted to kill him. That's how I know that McFarlane is the murderer. That young man has **evil** eyes, Mr Holmes, he has the eyes of a murderer.'

'Thank you, Mrs Lexington,' said Holmes. 'Is there anything more you can tell me? Anything that could help us with our investigation?'

'I can tell you this,' answered the housekeeper. 'The police found some buttons in those remains in the timber yard this morning. Those buttons are Mr Oldacre's. They're the buttons from his trousers. He was wearing them last night.'

upset yourself to make yourself feel unhappy

evil very bad

23

'You've been very helpful,' said Holmes. He stood up. 'But now I must go. Thank you for your time, Mrs Lexington.'

The housekeeper got up suddenly. 'I tried to save him, Mr Holmes, poor Mr Oldacre,' she said. 'I ran out into the timber yard, but the wood was so dry. It was burning so quickly. I can't remember the last time it rained. The smell was terrible . . . when I think . . .'

'Thank you, Mrs Lexington,' Holmes said once more. 'Goodbye.'

He closed the door behind him as he left the kitchen. In the hall he met Sergeant Judd, who was coming down the stairs.

'Mr Holmes,' said the policeman. 'I hope that your visit has been helpful.'

'Very helpful, Sergeant,' Holmes replied. 'Thank you. And I hope that your investigation is going well.'

'We have our murderer, Mr Holmes,' the policeman answered. 'Inspector Lestrade is talking to him now at Scotland Yard. His name is John Hector McFarlane and he killed Mr Oldacre for his house and his money.'

'I'm very pleased to hear that you have your man,' said Holmes with his strange smile. 'It's **obvious**, I'm sure, that Mr McFarlane murdered Jonas Oldacre and burnt his body in the timber yard.'

'I'm happy to hear that you agree, sir,' replied Judd. 'Goodbye, Mr Holmes.'

'Goodbye, Sergeant,' said Holmes.

He walked slowly to the front door, looking carefully at the walls in the hall, and left the builder's house. Outside he took a last look at the garden, house, and timber yard and **drew** a plan in his notebook before walking through the streets of Norwood to the station. It was a fine summer day, but Holmes wasn't happy.

In the train back to London, he asked himself a number of questions. Could John McFarlane really be a murderer? Was Jonas Oldacre really dead? Why did the builder suddenly decide to leave all his money to a young man that he didn't know? And why did he write his will on an express train? For now, Holmes did not know the answer to his questions, but he was sure that they were good questions to ask.

obvious easy to see or understand

draw (*past* **drew, drawn**) to make a picture with a pen or pencil

READING CHECK

Correct the mistakes in these sentences.

a Holmes finds Deep Dene House ~~with difficulty~~. *easily*

b The builder's house is small and modern.

c The police have found burnt remains in the garden.

d Sergeant Judd doesn't know Sherlock Holmes's name.

e Holmes says that he is helping Sergeant Judd with his investigation.

f The police have found keys from Oldacre's trousers in the ashes.

g Judd thinks that Oldacre is the murderer.

h In the bedroom Holmes finds bloodstains and fingerprints.

i Holmes finds out that Oldacre has a lot of money in the bank.

j Mrs Lexington is Jonas Oldacre's daughter.

k Mrs Lexington says that Oldacre is alive.

WORD WORK

1 Find ten words from Chapter 4 in the word square.

C	A	G	S	H	O	N	E	T	F
R	B	B	P	S	F	H	I	S	O
O	I	U	A	E	L	A	W	N	O
U	A	T	R	A	E	Y	A	Y	T
C	B	T	D	R	V	F	D	A	P
H	U	O	A	C	I	T	R	I	R
E	I	N	T	H	L	R	E	S	I
S	A	S	H	E	S	T	W	R	N
D	P	H	A	S	O	S	T	Y	T
O	F	X	H	K	D	E	E	D	S

ACTIVITIES

2 Use the words from Activity 1 to complete the sentences.

a The police think that the .... _ashes_ .... are Jonas Oldacre's body.

b Holmes spends more than an hour in the garden, looking at the ....

c Sergeant Judd's eyes .... excitedly.

d After looking at the garden, Holmes .... the house.

e The police find some trouser .... in the remains of the fire.

f There are .... on the bedroom floor.

g The .... to the house aren't in the safe.

h Mrs Lexington says that John McFarlane has

.... eyes.

i There are some bags of .... in the
timber yard.

j Holmes .... down to look at the
bedroom floor.

k Holmes .... a plan.

GUESS WHAT

What happens in the next chapter? Tick the boxes.   **Yes Perhaps No**

a Holmes arrives back at Baker Street in the middle of the night. ☐ ☐ ☐

b Watson is waiting for Holmes at Baker Street. ☐ ☐ ☐

c Holmes immediately tells Watson what he has done in
Blackheath and Norwood. ☐ ☐ ☐

d Holmes tells Watson that he thinks that John McFarlane is
a murderer. ☐ ☐ ☐

e Holmes tells Watson that Oldacre was a very rich man. ☐ ☐ ☐

f Watson starts to think that McFarlane murdered Oldacre for
his money. ☐ ☐ ☐

g Holmes spends the night thinking and smoking cigarettes. ☐ ☐ ☐

Chapter five

Who is Mr Cornelius?

It was early evening when Holmes arrived back at 221B Baker Street. Mrs Hudson opened the door to him and he followed her upstairs. Watson was waiting for him in their rooms.

'Holmes!' he cried. 'At last! Where have you been? I was worried.'

'No need to worry, Watson,' Holmes replied. 'I've been to Blackheath and also to Norwood.'

'You must tell me everything,' said Watson, who was very excited.

'Later,' answered Holmes. 'First I must think some more.'

'But Holmes . . . !' Watson shouted angrily.

Holmes held up a hand.

'I must think, Watson,' Holmes said again. He walked to the corner of the room and **picked up** his **violin**. Mrs Hudson left the room, shaking her head. Watson angrily started to read a book while Holmes began to play the violin.

He played for more than an hour, his eyes closed. Watson knew that his friend was thinking deeply. He had to wait until Holmes was ready to tell him about his visits to Blackheath and Norwood.

At last Holmes put his violin on the table and sat down.

'Watson,' he said, 'it has been a strange day. I have spoken to Mr McFarlane's mother and Mr Oldacre's housekeeper, a Mrs Lexington, and still I don't know what really happened at Deep Dene House last night. Perhaps our Mr McFarlane isn't innocent after all, but an evil murderer.'

'Do you really think that, Holmes?' asked Watson.

'No, Watson, I don't,' Holmes answered. 'I still think he's

pick up to take something in your hand

violin a musical instrument, made of wood with strings across it

innocent. But, as Inspector Lestrade tells us, he had a good motive for killing Jonas Oldacre and he was at Deep Dene House yesterday evening.'

'What did you learn from his mother, Holmes?' said Watson.

'I learned something very interesting,' replied Holmes. 'I learned that Oldacre once asked her to marry him.'

'Really?'

'Really,' said Holmes. 'And he was very unhappy when she said no to him. He was so angry that he sent her a photograph of herself which was slashed with a knife across her face. Mrs McFarlane was a very beautiful young woman, Watson. It isn't difficult to understand why the builder was so hurt when she married another man, a man with no money. The photograph arrived on the day that she married John McFarlane's father.'

'Oh dear!' said Watson. 'So Oldacre was unlucky in love.'

'Yes,' Holmes agreed. 'But it is strange that he wanted to leave everything that he had to Mrs McFarlane's son. Very strange.'

'Was Mrs McFarlane surprised?' asked Watson.

'"I want nothing from Mr Jonas Oldacre," she said,' Holmes replied, '"and my son wants nothing from him. I am happy that he is dead." I understand how she feels, Watson. She's a good woman, I am sure, too good for Mr Jonas Oldacre.'

'Did she tell you more about him?'

'No, nothing more,' said Holmes. 'Next I travelled to Norwood, to Deep Dene House, to see for myself the place where the builder met his death. It's a big, modern house with a large garden. There are a lot of trees.'

'So Oldacre was a very rich man,' Watson suggested.

'He had a large house and a large garden,' Holmes replied, 'but he wasn't so rich after all. I saw his bank book.' Here

Holmes opened the cigarette box on the table and took out a cigarette. He gave his friend a short time to think about his words before he lit it.

'I see,' said Watson at last.

'Do you?' asked Holmes. 'I'm not sure I see yet. But I must go on with my story. As I said, Oldacre's house was large and modern, and next to it was the famous timber yard.' He took out his notebook and opened it on the table in front of him. 'Here, Watson, I drew a plan of it.'

Watson got up and walked across the room to stand behind Holmes and look at the plan.

'You see,' Holmes went on, 'this is the Sydenham Road, here is Deep Dene House and this is the timber yard. On the left are the French windows which open into the builder's bedroom. As you can see, it's possible to look into the bedroom from the road.'

'Is that important, Holmes?' asked Watson.

'I don't know,' Holmes replied. 'Possibly. Inspector Lestrade wasn't at Norwood this afternoon, but I met his sergeant, a man called Judd. He, of course, was quite sure that our Mr McFarlane is a murderer. The police found some buttons in the ashes in the timber yard, you see, and these buttons were buttons from Oldacre's trousers. And so, says Sergeant Judd, the builder is dead, and so McFarlane is a murderer.'

'This doesn't look good, Holmes,' said Watson.

'No,' Holmes agreed. 'Our young friend is in deep trouble here, I'm afraid. But we must not **give up** hope, Watson. I searched the garden after talking to Sergeant Judd, but I found nothing. Then I went into the house. First I searched the builder's bedroom. The bloodstains on the walls were **fresh**, and I saw Oldacre's footprints on the floor, together with John McFarlane's. But there were no others. I looked at the papers from the safe, which were on the table, but I'm sure that some of the papers were not there. I couldn't find the deeds to the house anywhere.'

'Where do you think they are, Holmes?' asked Watson.

'I don't know. But I'm sure that our young friend didn't take them. He had no **reason** to steal the deeds if Oldacre wanted to leave his house and money to him. Well, Watson, next I spoke to the builder's housekeeper, Mrs Lexington. A small, quiet woman, she never looked at me once when she was talking to me. I am sure that she knows much more than she wanted to tell me. She agreed that she answered the front door to John McFarlane at nine thirty yesterday evening. She went to bed at ten thirty – her bedroom is

give up (*past* **gave**, **given**) to stop trying to do something

fresh made not long ago; not old

reason why you do something

at the other end of the house – and fell asleep. She woke up later and smelled smoke from the fire. She got up and searched everywhere for Oldacre, but she couldn't find him. Of course, she thinks that this is because he was dead, murdered.'

'What did she say about the builder?' asked Watson.

Holmes held up his hand. 'A good man, she told me. He had enemies, of course, as everyone has enemies, but his life at Norwood was a quiet one. Nobody wanted him dead – only his murderer, our friend McFarlane. He has evil eyes, she tells me, Watson.'

'Evil eyes?' Watson replied. 'Was the woman **mad**?'

'Not mad, Watson,' said Holmes, 'but also not very helpful. Mrs Lexington told me very little. As I said, I am sure that she knows more.'

'Did you find out nothing at Norwood that could help McFarlane?' asked Watson.

Holmes looked thoughtful. 'Possibly,' he said at last. 'You remember I said that I saw Oldacre's bank book and that it showed that he was not as rich as everybody thought?'

Watson **nodded**.

'Well,' Holmes went on, 'when I looked at his **chequebook** I found that he wrote a lot of cheques to someone called Mr Cornelius. These were cheques for a lot of money. Who is this Mr Cornelius, Watson? And why did our builder pay him so much money? That is what I want to know.'

'This could help our young friend and prove to Lestrade that he is not a murderer, that he is innocent,' cried Watson, excited by Holmes' news.

'Perhaps, Watson,' Holmes agreed. 'But for now we have nothing more while Lestrade has McFarlane's visit to Oldacre, the buttons from the builder's trousers in the ashes in the timber yard and Mrs Lexington's story. I must say, Watson, I do not feel hopeful.'

mad not thinking well

nod to move your head up and down

chequebook a book with pieces of paper that you can write on and use to pay for things

Holmes put out his cigarette and picked up his violin again. Watson ate dinner alone that night and went to bed early. Holmes did not go to bed at all. He spent the night playing the violin, smoking cigarette after cigarette and thinking about John McFarlane and Jonas Oldacre. In the end, as the sun came up the next morning, he fell asleep in his chair.

READING CHECK

Are these sentences true or false? Tick the boxes.

		True	False
a	Mrs Hudson opens the door to Sherlock Holmes when he arrives back at 221B Baker Street.	☑	☐
b	Watson is very pleased to see Holmes.	☐	☐
c	Watson reads the newspaper while Holmes plays the violin.	☐	☐
d	Watson decides that John McFarlane is an evil murderer.	☐	☐
e	Holmes tells Watson that Oldacre once asked McFarlane's mother to marry him.	☐	☐
f	Holmes shows Watson his plan of Deep Dene House.	☐	☐
g	Holmes tells Watson that the deeds to the house were in the builder's safe.	☐	☐
h	Watson agrees that McFarlane has evil eyes.	☐	☐
i	Holmes wants to know who Mr Cornelius is.	☐	☐
j	Holmes feels hopeful for John McFarlane.	☐	☐
k	Holmes does not sleep until morning.	☐	☐

WORD WORK

Complete the words to make sentences about the story.
All of the words come from Chapter 5.

a Watson angrily starts to read a book when Holmes $\underline{P}i\underline{ck}\underline{s}$ $\underline{u}$p his _ i _ _ i _ .

b McFarlane has an obvious _ e_ _ o _ for killing Oldacre – his money.

c Holmes saw the name 'Mr Cornelius' in Oldacre's _ _ _ q _ _ b _ _ k.

d Watson doesn't say 'yes' but he _ o _ _ at what Holmes says.

e The bloodstains on the wall weren't old. They were _ _e_ _ .

f Holmes doesn't want to _ i _ _ u _ hope that McFarlane is innocent.

g Watson thinks Mrs Lexington is _ a _ .

GUESS WHAT

What happens in the next chapter? Tick the boxes.

1 Watson...

a ☐ wakes up very late the next day.

b ☐ finds Holmes asleep in his chair.

c ☐ has breakfast with Inspector Lestrade.

2 Holmes...

a ☐ decides that McFarlane is not innocent.

b ☐ goes to Norwood to meet Lestrade.

c ☐ goes back to Blackheath to see Mrs McFarlane.

3 Lestrade...

a ☐ tells Holmes why he is sure that McFarlane murdered Oldacre.

b ☐ tells McFarlane that he is a murderer.

c ☐ visits John McFarlane's mother and father.

Chapter six

A thumbprint on the wall

W atson was surprised to find his friend fast asleep when he came down to breakfast the next morning. He shook him **gently**.

'Wake up,' he said. 'Mrs Hudson will be here soon.'

Holmes woke up immediately. 'Good morning, Watson,' he replied. He saw the questions in the doctor's eyes before he could ask them. 'Yes, I have been here all night. Yes, I have slept very little. And no, I do not know how we can save our young friend, John McFarlane.'

'Oh,' said Watson, 'then perhaps you should wash and change before breakfast.'

'You're right, Watson,' Holmes agreed. He left the room, and Watson sat down at the table. Soon after Mrs Hudson came in with the morning newspaper and a **telegram**.

'Good morning, Dr Watson,' she said. 'Here's your newspaper, and this telegram has just arrived for Mr Holmes. It looks very important.'

Watson took the telegram and looked at it thoughtfully.

'I'm sure it is very important,' he agreed. 'Perhaps it's about Mr McFarlane.'

'The young man who came here yesterday morning?'

'That's right,' said Watson. 'Inspector Lestrade is convinced that he's a murderer, but Holmes and I don't agree.'

'A murderer?' the housekeeper replied. 'Well, he was a strange young man – so wild and excited. But a murderer? I don't think so.'

'Mrs Hudson, your **opinion** is good enough for me,' said Watson. 'Now is that my breakfast that I can smell?'

The housekeeper smiled. 'You're always ready for your breakfast, Dr Watson,' she said. 'It'll be about ten minutes.'

As Mrs Hudson left the room, Holmes returned. He

gently softly

telegram a very short letter that you send very quickly

opinion what you think about someone or something

immediately saw the telegram in Watson's hand.

'That looks interesting,' he said. 'For me?'

Watson nodded and gave him the telegram. Holmes opened it with a paper knife and read it silently. He said nothing but looked out of the window onto Baker Street.

'Well?' asked Watson when he could wait no longer.

Holmes turned to look at his friend 'It's from Lestrade. The Inspector is at Deep Dene House at the moment. He says he has **proof** that McFarlane is the murderer of Jonas Oldacre. In his opinion, we should now give up.'

'This doesn't look good, Holmes,' said Watson.

To his surprise, Holmes laughed.

'Inspector Lestrade has always been sure that John McFarlane killed the builder,' he said, 'and now he says that he has proof. Well, let's see his proof. This is not the time to give up, Watson. We'll go to Norwood immediately.'

'But Holmes,' said Watson, 'it's still very early and—'

Just then Mrs Hudson arrived with their breakfasts.

'And you haven't had your breakfast,' Holmes went on with a smile. 'All right, Watson, we'll go after breakfast. I'm sure that Inspector Lestrade's proof can wait.'

Holmes ate nothing himself, so Watson enjoyed a very large meal and it was after nine o'clock when they left Baker Street. They took a **cab** to the station and it was not long before they were at the front door of Deep Dene House. Watson rang the **doorbell**.

'Now, Watson,' said Holmes, 'you will meet the silent Mrs Lexington.'

A moment later the door opened and the housekeeper stood in front of them.

'Mr Holmes,' she said. 'How can I help you?'

'Good morning to you, Mrs Lexington,' said Holmes. 'This is my good friend, Dr Watson. Is Inspector Lestrade here?'

'He is,' the housekeeper replied.

proof information that shows that something is really true

cab a taxi

doorbell the bell on the front door

37

thumbprint the mark that your thumb makes when it touches something

'Please take us to him.'

Holmes and Watson went in and followed Mrs Lexington to the back of the house. Lestrade was sitting at a table. He looked very pleased to see them.

'Mr Holmes, Dr Watson! Good morning!' he said, standing up. 'You've come to see my proof, I suppose.'

'That's right,' Holmes agreed with a smile. 'I am very happy for you, Lestrade, that you were right all the time.'

'It's good of you to agree that you were wrong,' said the Inspector. 'As for me, I never thought that McFarlane was innocent. The man is a murderer.'

'I'm sure that you are right, Inspector,' Holmes agreed, 'but perhaps we can see your proof now.'

'Of course,' said Lestrade. 'Come with me.'

He stood up and Holmes and Watson followed him into the hall.

'Here,' said the Inspector. 'Look at this.'

Holmes and Watson crouched down to look at a bloodstain on the wall.

'It's a **thumbprint**,' Lestrade explained. 'John McFarlane's thumbprint.'

'Are you sure?' asked Watson.

'Oh yes,' Lestrade replied. 'That is John McFarlane's thumbprint. I'm sorry, Dr Watson, but your young friend killed Jonas Oldacre. He will die for this crime.'

Holmes looked very thoughtful.

'You're very quiet, Mr Holmes,' said the Inspector. 'Do you have nothing to say?'

Holmes stood up. 'As I said before, Inspector, it's obvious that you are right about McFarlane. He killed the builder for his money and his house. I have only two questions.'

'Go on,' said Lestrade, who was no longer smiling.

'First,' said Holmes, 'who found this thumbprint?'

'It was Mrs Lexington, the housekeeper, who saw it first,' the Inspector replied. 'She showed it to Sergeant Judd.'

'Really?' Holmes looked very pleased with this answer.

'What's your second question, Mr Holmes?' asked Lestrade.

'Why didn't your men find the thumbprint yesterday?'

'That's easy to explain,' the Inspector replied. 'They weren't looking for thumbprints yesterday, not in the hall. And the thumbprint is a little hard to see.'

'Yes, it's hard to see,' Holmes agreed. 'Watson and I had to crouch down to see it. But Mrs Lexington saw it. Perhaps she was washing the floor. I suppose that you are sure that the thumbprint was here yesterday, Inspector?'

'Of course it was!' Lestrade replied crossly. 'Do you think that McFarlane left Scotland Yard during the night and came here to make a thumbprint in blood on the wall?'

'Perhaps not,' said Holmes thoughtfully.

'Then I must ask you both to excuse me. I must return to Scotland Yard to talk to the murderer.'

Lestrade left the room.

'So John McFarlane is a murderer,' said Watson sadly.

'I don't think so, Watson,' Holmes replied.

'What? But Lestrade's proof – the thumbprint! How do you explain it, Holmes?'

'It's impossible to explain,' said Holmes, 'and for a very good reason. There was no thumbprint on this wall when I was here yesterday.'

READING CHECK

Correct eleven more mistakes in the story.

Watson is surprised to find Holmes ~~awake~~ *asleep* when he
comes down to breakfast the next morning. Holmes has
slept very little. Mrs Hudson arrives with the newspaper
and a letter for Holmes. When Holmes is out of the
room, Mrs Hudson and Watson talk about Jonas Oldacre.
Inspector Lestrade has written from Blackheath to say he
is now sure that McFarlane killed the builder and wants
Holmes and Watson to go on with their investigation.

Holmes and Watson take a cab to Norwood. Sergeant
Judd opens the door of Deep Dene House. Lestrade
shows Holmes McFarlane's fingerprint on the floor. But
Sergeant Judd found it earlier that day and showed it to
Lestrade. Holmes is convinced by Lestrade's proof.

WORD WORK

**Match the words in the violin with the underlined words in the sentences on
page 41.**

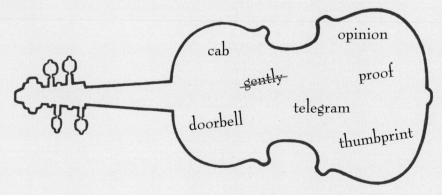

opinion

cab

~~gently~~

proof

doorbell

telegram

thumbprint

a Watson shook Holmes <u>in a quiet kind way</u> to wake him. ..... *gently*.....

b Lestrade sent a <u>fast letter by electric wires</u> to Holmes. ....

c Lestrade's <u>way of thinking</u> is that McFarlane is Oldacre's murderer. ....

d Listen. It's the <u>bell on the door</u>! I'll go and see who it is. ....

e Lestrade says that McFarlane killed the builder, and that he has now got <u>something that shows his idea is true</u>. ....

f Watson and Holmes take a <u>taxi with horses pulling it</u> to the station. ....

g This glass is dirty; there's a <u>mark from someone's thumb</u> on it. ....

GUESS WHAT

What happens in the next chapter? Tick six boxes.

a ☐ John McFarlane goes back to Deep Dene House.

b ☐ Holmes understands why the thumbprint is important.

c ☐ Watson decides that McFarlane is a murderer.

d ☐ Holmes and Watson go into the garden to look at Oldacre's house.

e ☐ Inspector Lestrade writes about the murder.

f ☐ Holmes asks Watson to start a fire in the house.

g ☐ The police find a woman in a secret room.

h ☐ Holmes finds Jonas Oldacre's murderer.

i ☐ Lestrade agrees that Holmes is right about John McFarlane.

j ☐ The police decide to arrest Mrs Lexington.

Chapter seven

The man on the top floor

W atson did not know what to think.

'I don't understand this, Holmes,' he said at last. 'I don't understand this at all. If the thumbprint wasn't here yesterday—'

Holmes held up a hand to stop him.

'There are two possibilities, Watson. The first is that John McFarlane left his **cell** at Scotland Yard during the night, took the train to Norwood and came to Deep Dene Lodge to make a bloody thumbprint on the wall here. I do not think this is very **probable**, Watson, do you?'

'Of course not, Holmes,' said Watson.

'Then you and I and Inspector Lestrade have the same opinion, and it was not John McFarlane who left this thumbprint.'

'But Lestrade said that it was McFarlane's thumbprint!' said Watson excitedly.

'Oh I am sure that it is McFarlane's thumbprint,' Holmes replied, 'but I am also sure that it was not John McFarlane who left it here. Come, Watson.'

Dr Watson followed his friend out into the garden.

'What are we doing, Holmes?' he asked.

'We're looking,' said Holmes, 'we're looking very carefully.'

Holmes stood in the garden and looked thoughtfully at the front of the house. Then he walked across the lawn and looked at the side of the house. Next Watson followed him to the back of the house and then to the other side, which looked onto the Sydenham Road. Here Holmes stood for a long time with a look of great interest on his face.

'Good,' he said at last, and walked quickly back to the front door, which was still open. Watson followed him inside and downstairs into the **basement**. Holmes looked very carefully

cell a small room in a prison or police station

probable almost certainly true

basement downstairs from the ground floor of a house

in every room on that floor, then did the same on the ground floor. There was no **furniture** in many of the rooms, but Holmes looked thoughtfully at the walls and at the floor. He and Watson then went upstairs and visited all the bedrooms and the bathroom. After that they climbed to the top floor of the house, where there were three bedrooms, all empty. Holmes began to laugh. He laughed and laughed. Watson looked at his friend, astonished.

'Holmes, what is it?' he asked. 'Are you not feeling well?'

Holmes stopped laughing at once and turned to Watson.

'I'm feeling very well, Watson,' he said with a strange smile. 'Come, let us find Inspector Lestrade.'

They went downstairs and found the Inspector at his table. He was busy writing his **report**.

'Are you writing your report already, Inspector?' asked Holmes. 'Are you so sure that you have your murderer?'

Lestrade stopped writing and put down his pen. He did not look pleased.

'Mr Holmes, I have shown you my proof. John McFarlane's thumbprint **proves** that he killed Jonas Oldacre. I have my murderer. He is in his cell at Scotland Yard as we speak.'

'I think, Inspector,' said Holmes, 'that you should speak to one more person before you finish writing your report.'

'Who is this person?' asked Lestrade. 'And where can I find him?'

'How many policemen do you have here today, Inspector?'

Lestrade was surprised, but he answered immediately.

'Sergeant Judd and two others.'

'And are they all big, strong men with loud voices?'

Lestrade looked at Watson. Watson looked at Lestrade. They were both **baffled**.

'They are all tall and I'm sure that they can shout very loudly if they need to,' the Inspector replied, 'but I don't understand—'

furniture tables and chairs for example

report what someone writes to explain something that has happened

prove to show that something is certainly true

baffled when you don't understand something

43

Holmes held up a hand.

'You will understand, Inspector. Now could you please call your men?'

It was obvious that Lestrade was not happy, but he left the room and went to look for Sergeant Judd and the others. Five minutes later Holmes and Watson found Lestrade in the hall with his men.

'Sergeant Judd, you will find some hay in the timber yard. Could you please bring it into the house?' asked Holmes.

Judd looked at Lestrade, who nodded. He came back a few minutes later with a bag of hay.

'This will help us to find our man,' said Holmes. 'Now, Watson, do you have any **matches** in your pocket?'

Watson nodded.

'Then we are ready. Follow me, please.'

The policemen followed Holmes and Watson as they climbed the stairs to the top of the house. When they arrived, Lestrade's face was very red.

'What are you doing, Mr Holmes?' he asked crossly. 'I hope that this is not a **joke**.'

'You will not have to wait much longer, Inspector,' said Holmes with a smile. 'Could you please ask one of your men to bring some water from the bathroom?'

'Water!' Lestrade replied. 'Mr Holmes, I really must . . . '

'Please, Inspector.'

Lestrade thought for a long moment, but in the end sent one of his men to the bathroom for water. When he returned, Holmes opened a window and then asked Watson to light the hay with a match. The hay caught fire immediately and suddenly there was smoke everywhere.

'Now we will find our man, Lestrade,' said Holmes. 'Could we all please shout "fire"? One, two, three . . . '

Holmes, Watson and the four policemen all shouted 'fire!' in loud voices.

match you use this to light a fire

joke something that you do to make people laugh

'Again!' said Holmes.

'Fire!'

'And again!'

'Fire!' This time the shout was so loud that Lestrade put his fingers in his ears. Just then a very strange thing happened: a secret door in the wall opened suddenly and a little man ran out.

'Here's your man, Inspector,' said Holmes with a laugh. 'Sergeant Judd, please put some water on the hay to put out our little fire. Thank you. Inspector, this is Mr Jonas Oldacre, the Norwood builder. I think we will learn that he also has another name – Mr Cornelius.'

Watson and the policemen looked long and hard at the

little man, who was standing in front of them and shaking. He had grey eyes and white hair and was very **ugly**.

'Well,' said Lestrade at last when the fire was out. 'Do you have nothing to say, Mr Jonas Oldacre?'

Lestrade's face was red and angry. Oldacre looked very afraid, but he laughed excitedly.

'It was a joke, Inspector,' he explained. 'No more. I never wanted to make any trouble for anybody.'

'What?' said Lestrade angrily. 'You didn't want to make any trouble? And an innocent man is in the cells at Scotland Yard as we speak!'

'Just my little joke, Inspector,' the builder said again.

'Take him away, Sergeant,' said Lestrade. 'The man is dangerous.'

Oldacre went downstairs with Judd and the other policemen. Lestrade turned to Holmes.

'Well, Mr Holmes, once again I have to thank you. This time I was wrong and you were right. John McFarlane is an innocent man. It's obvious that there was no murder here.'

'That's right, Inspector,' Holmes smiled, 'but I understand your mistake. Jonas Oldacre was very clever.'

'But Sherlock Holmes was cleverer!' said Watson. 'Very good work, Holmes.'

'Thank you, Watson. Now let's see the secret room.'

Watson and Lestrade followed Holmes into the room, which was about two metres long. It was impossible to see the door from the **passage**, but in the room they found some furniture, food and water, newspapers and books. Holmes picked up a newspaper.

'This morning's newspaper,' he said. 'I'm sure that Oldacre has enjoyed reading about Mr McFarlane's arrest. And I suppose that Mrs Lexington is the person who has brought him his newspapers and his food and drink.'

ugly not beautiful

passage the space between rooms in a house

'I must speak to that woman again,' said Lestrade. 'I always thought she had her secrets.'

'Perhaps she has a very big secret,' said Holmes. 'Perhaps she is more to Mr Oldacre than a housekeeper.'

Lestrade looked thoughtful. 'Of course,' he said at last. 'That's why she was happy to **tell lies** for him. She will go to **prison** for this, Mr Holmes.'

'Very good,' Holmes replied. 'Norwood will be a better place without her.'

'I have just one more question for you, Mr Holmes,' said Lestrade. 'Why did Oldacre do this? Why did he want me to arrest John McFarlane?'

Holmes gave the Inspector a long look.

'Many years ago, Inspector,' he explained, 'Jonas Oldacre fell in love. He fell in love with John McFarlane's mother. They spent some time together, but Mrs McFarlane saw that Oldacre was cruel and dangerous and she sent him away. Later she married John's father. On the day that they married Oldacre sent her a photograph of herself with her face slashed. He was very angry and he never forgot it.'

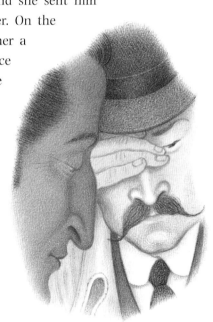

'I see,' said Lestrade. 'So that's why you went to Blackheath.'

'I wanted to talk to John's parents,' Holmes explained. 'I couldn't understand why Oldacre wanted to leave everything to John in his will.'

'I've been very stupid,' said Lestrade sadly.

'Not at all,' said Watson kindly. 'But Sherlock Holmes has been very clever.'

Holmes himself said nothing.

tell lies to say things which are not true

prison a place where people must stay when they do something wrong

READING CHECK

What do they say?

① What are we doing?

② Take him away.

③ Could we all please shout 'fire'?

④ Do you have nothing to say?

⑤ It was a joke.

⑥ Are you writing your report already?

⑦ John McFarlane's thumbprint proves that he killed Jonas

⑧ It was not John McFarlane who left this thumbprint.

⑨ You will find some hay in the timber yard.

⑩ I think that you should speak to one more person.

a Holmes tells Watson: It was not John McFarlane who left this thumbprint.

b Watson asks Holmes: ....

c Holmes asks Lestrade: ....

d Lestrade tells Holmes: ....

e Holmes tells Lestrade: ....

f Holmes tells Sergeant Judd: ....

g Holmes asks Watson and the policemen: ....

h Lestrade asks Oldacre: ....

i Oldacre tells Lestrade: ....

j Lestrade says to Sergeant Judd: ....

WORD WORK

1 Find words from Chapter 7.

a BABLEROP probable

b TURINFURE ....

c FLEDFAB ....

d SHETMAC ....

e LELC ....

f MANSEBET ....

g ROTERP ....

h EVROP ....

i KEOJ ....

j SAPGESA ....

2 Complete the sentences with the words from Activity 1.

a Holmes did not think that it was . probable . that John McFarlane made the thumbprint.

b Lestrade thought that he could .... that John McFarlane was a murderer.

c He was writing a .... about the murder of Jonas Oldacre when Holmes stopped him.

d A .... is a room under the ground at the bottom of a house.

e There was no .... in many of the rooms in the house.

f Lestrade and Watson were .... when Holmes asked about the policemen's voices. They couldn't understand why he was asking.

g Watson used .... and dry hay to light a fire.

h Holmes knew there was a secret room behind one of the walls in the ....

i It is not a .... when a criminal sends an innocent man to prison for something he didn't do.

j Oldacre will spend some time in a prison ....

GUESS WHAT

What happens in the next chapter? Match the first and second parts of these sentences.

a	John McFarlane	**1**	take a cab to Scotland Yard.
b	Sherlock Holmes explains	**2**	that Holmes has been very helpful.
c	Holmes, Watson and McFarlane	**3**	visits Holmes and Watson in Baker Street.
d	Watson asks Holmes	**4**	for saving the life of an innocent man.
e	Inspector Lestrade agrees	**5**	why they are going to see Inspector Lestrade.
f	Lestrade thanks Holmes	**6**	how he realized that Jonas Oldacre was not dead.

Chapter eight

A free man

T wo days later, on a fine summer morning, Holmes and
Watson were sitting once again in their Baker Street
rooms. Watson was reading the newspaper excitedly.

'It's here, Holmes!' he cried. 'The story of our Norwood
builder. Listen to this: *Inspector Lestrade of Scotland Yard*
realized *that Jonas Oldacre was still alive and found him on
the top floor of his house, Deep Dene Lodge at Norwood, where
he was hiding in a secret room.* But Lestrade realized nothing
at all, Holmes! This is terrible. If you—'

'It's not important, Watson,' said Holmes quietly. 'What
is important is that Oldacre will go to prison and John
McFarlane will not die for a crime that he didn't **commit**.
Lestrade knows what really happened, after all.'

'I don't understand how you can be so **calm** about this,'
said Watson crossly. 'It was you who realized that the builder
wasn't dead, not Lestrade. Lestrade was convinced that John
McFarlane was a murderer.'

Just then the door opened and Mrs Hudson came in.

'A young man to see you, Mr Holmes,' she said with a
smile.

John McFarlane walked into the room. He looked calm
and very happy. Holmes and Watson stood up.

'Mr McFarlane,' said Holmes, 'I'm very pleased to see you.'

'Mr Holmes, Dr Watson, what can I say?' McFarlane replied.
'Thank you so much for everything. You have saved my life.
The police were convinced that I killed Jonas Oldacre.'

Watson asked the young man to sit down, and Mrs Hudson
left them. Holmes lit a cigarette from the box on the table.

'I was sure that I would die,' McFarlane went on. 'I was
at Deep Dene House. I had a very good motive. And when
the police found my thumbprint on the wall . . . Please tell

realize to suddenly
understand
something

commit to do a
crime

calm not worried

me, Mr Holmes, how you proved to Inspector Lestrade that I was innocent of this crime.'

Holmes did not speak for a long moment. He looked very thoughtful.

'It was a long time before I realized that there was no murder, but when I realized this, I understood everything. Oldacre once loved your mother and was very angry when she married another man. He had a lot of trouble with his business last year and lost a lot of money. His plan was to **disappear**, with Mrs Lexington perhaps, and start a new life with a different name: Mr Cornelius. He wanted everyone to think that he was dead because he didn't want anyone to look for him. And he wanted to hurt your mother and father. He wanted you to die for a crime that never happened.'

'But the burnt remains in the timber yard – what were they?' McFarlane wanted to know.

'A dead dog, I think,' Holmes replied. 'Not a dead builder.'

'What an evil man!' cried McFarlane. 'My mother was right to say no when he asked her to marry him.'

'Oh yes,' Holmes agreed. 'Jonas Oldacre is a very bad man and I hope that he will go to prison for a very long time.'

'I don't know how to thank you, Mr Holmes,' said McFarlane. 'I am so pleased that I came to you in my trouble.'

Holmes put out his cigarette and turned to Watson.

'Are we free this morning, Watson?' he asked.

'Yes,' his friend replied in surprise. 'Why do you ask?'

'It's a beautiful morning,' said Holmes. 'Let's go out.'

Watson and McFarlane followed Holmes down the stairs and out into Baker Street. The sun was shining and the streets of London were warm.

'A beautiful morning,' Holmes said once again. 'Watson, please find us a cab.'

disappear to go away suddenly

Ten minutes later the three men were in a cab and travelling south towards Scotland Yard.

'Why are we going to Scotland Yard, Holmes?' asked Watson.

'I'm sure that our good friend, inspector Lestrade, has something to say to Mr McFarlane,' Holmes replied.

At Scotland Yard they found Lestrade in his office. He looked surprised to see them.

'I was just finishing my report,' he explained.

'I thought that you might have something to say to Mr McFarlane, Inspector,' said Holmes as the young man followed the detective and Dr Watson into Lestrade's office.

'Oh, of course,' Lestrade agreed. He didn't look very happy. 'Mr McFarlane, I am very sorry that I thought that you were a murderer. I was wrong, of course, and Mr Holmes was right. I hope that the time you spent here at Scotland Yard wasn't too **unpleasant.**'

'It wasn't the happiest time of my life,' McFarlane replied, 'but the important thing is that I am now a free man – **thanks to** Mr Sherlock Holmes.'

'Yes, Mr Holmes has been very helpful, once again,' said Lestrade. 'We work very well together, Mr Holmes and I.'

Holmes smiled. Watson looked angry, but said nothing.

'Mr Holmes, as you're here,' the Inspector went on, 'and I'm writing my report, I have one more question for you. Why was Mr McFarlane's thumbprint on the wall?'

'Oldacre put it there,' Holmes explained. 'When he and Mr McFarlane were working on his papers he asked Mr McFarlane to **seal** a letter with **wax**.

He then had John's thumbprint in the wax and he put this on the wall with some of his own blood.'

'Very clever,' said Lestrade.

'Yes,' Holmes agreed. 'His only problem was that I knew that the thumbprint wasn't there the day before. As Mr

unpleasant not nice

thanks to because of

seal to close by sticking two parts together

wax candles are made of wax

McFarlane was in a cell here at Scotland Yard, he didn't put it there, so I asked myself who did. The answer to the mystery was obvious. Oldacre, of course. And how is the Norwood builder?'

guilty who has done something wrong

'He's not a happy man,' said Lestrade, smiling at last. 'It was all a joke, he says. And of course he didn't want to hurt Mr McFarlane here.'

'A strange joke!' said Dr Watson.

'Yes,' Holmes agreed, 'it's a very strange joke that sends a man to his death!'

'I have to thank you, Mr Holmes,' said Lestrade, 'for saving the life of an innocent man.'

Holmes smiled.

'That is my business, Inspector: to save innocent people and make sure that those who are **guilty** go to prison. As long as I can do that, I will be a happy man.'

READING CHECK

Tick the correct pictures.

a . . . sees the story of the Norwood builder in the newspaper.

☐ Sherlock Holmes ☑ Doctor Watson

b Mrs Hudson opens the door to . . . .

☐ Inspector Lestrade   ☐ John McFarlane

c Holmes explains that Mr Cornelius is . . . .

☐ Jonas Oldacre   ☐ John McFarlane's father

d The builder planned to disappear with . . . .

☐ Mrs McFarlane   ☐ Mrs Lexington

e At Scotland Yard Holmes, Watson and McFarlane find . . . .

☐ Lestrade in his office   ☐ Judd in his office

f Holmes explains that . . . put the bloody thumbprint on the wall.

☐ Jonas Oldacre   ☐ Mrs Lexington

WORD WORK

Use the words in the prison cell to complete John McFarlane's diary.

25 August 1894

I leave Scotland Yard today a (1) calm man. I will not go to prison for a murder that I didn't (2) ...., and all (3) .... Mr Sherlock Holmes. He cleverly (4) .... that Oldacre was an (5) .... man who hated me and my parents. He understood that Oldacre wanted to (6) .... after his 'death' as Mr Cornelius, and that he used the thumbprint I made in the (7) .... when I (8) .... his will to put a bloody thumbprint on the wall.. Now Mr Holmes has convinced Inspector Lestrade that I am not (9) .... I can go home, a free man!

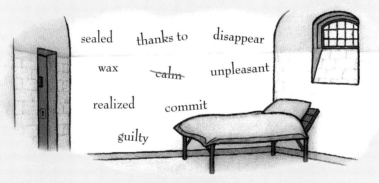

sealed thanks to disappear

wax calm unpleasant

realized commit

guilty

GUESS WHAT

What happens after the story ends? Choose from these ideas or add your own.

a ☐ Sherlock Holmes investigates another crime.

b ☐ Jonas Oldacre and Mrs Lexington go to prison.

c ☐ John McFarlane sells his story to the newspapers.

d ☐ Inspector Lestrade writes a report explaining how he always knew McFarlane was really innocent.

e ☐ McFarlane's parents invite Holmes and Watson to dinner.

f ☐ Doctor Watson realizes that Lestrade is not a bad policeman.

Project A   *A Visitors' Guide*

1 Look at the map and make sentences about the places in *The Norwood Mystery*.

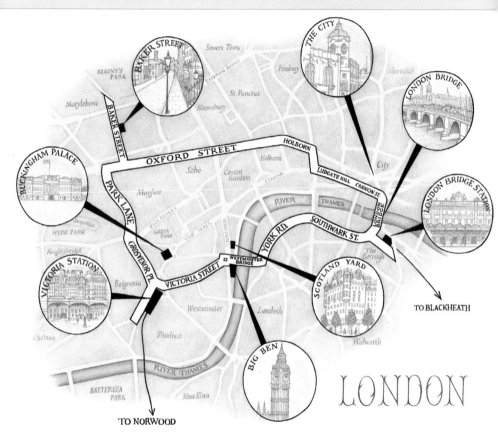

a <u>Sherlock Holmes and Doctor Watson live and work in</u> Baker Street.

b .... London Bridge Station.

c .... the City.

d .... Blackheath.

e .... Norwood.

f .... Scotland Yard.

2 Complete the text with the words below.

If you visit London in 1895 . . .

Never talk to men (1)................. show you the way,
try to sell you cigarettes or (2)................. a drink.

If you don't (3)................., go into a shop and ask,
or find a policeman.

Walk past anyone (4)................. for money and
don't walk along quiet streets after dark. Don't
(5)................. where poor people live.

Don't carry (6)................. with you. Be very
careful with your money when you go to the theatre
(7)................., when you are on the bus, and when
you are in the street.

Enjoy your visit!

a a lot of money   c or to church   e invite you for   g go to places
b who want to   d know the way   f who asks you

3 Now write about your village, town or city. Start like this:

If you visit .... in _ _ _ _ ...

Never ....

Project B   *An Author's Biography*

1 Read about Arthur Conan Doyle's life.

Arthur Conan Doyle was born in Edinburgh in 1859. At school he was not a good student, but he read a lot of books. When he was sixteen, he went to study in Austria for a year.

Arthur was strong and good at sport. When he left school, he went to Edinburgh University to study to be a doctor. His favourite teacher was a man called Joseph Bell, who showed him how to use his eyes like a good detective.

While he was a student, Conan Doyle was very poor, so he wrote stories to make money. He left the University in 1881 and worked as a doctor on a ship.

Conan Doyle was a good doctor, but he did not make much money. He started to write stories again. He remembered his lessons with Joseph Bell in Edinburgh and wrote a detective story, *A Study in Scarlet*. Sherlock Holmes was born! Conan Doyle went on to write fifty-nine more stories about his detective.

2 Correct the factual mistakes in the notes below.

Sir Arthur Conan Doyle
- born 1869, good student, read a lot
- studied in Austria for 16 years
- good at sport
- studied to be doctor at Oxford University
- favourite teacher Alexander Graham Bell
- as student started writing stories because needed money
- worked as doctor in hospital
- good doctor, made lots of money
- first Sherlock Holmes story was 'A Study in Scarlet'
- wrote 59 Sherlock Holmes stories in all

3 Read the biographical notes about another detective story writer – Alexander
   McCall Smith. Write a biography about him based on Conan Doyle's biography.

Alexander McCall Smith

- born Zimbabwe (then Rhodesia) in 1948
- educated Zimbabwe and Scotland
- lived in Botswana (Africa) for some years
- worked as Professor of Law at Botswana University
- until 2004 worked as Professor of Medical Law at Edinburgh
  University, lives in Edinburgh with family and cat, Gordon
- wrote 'No. 1 Ladies Detective Agency' in 1996 published in 1998
- has written over 50 books in all
- married wife, a doctor, Elizabeth Parry in 1982
- has 2 daughters – Lucy and Emily
- in free time plays bassoon in amateur orchestra
  'The Really Terrible Orchestra' (his wife plays flute)
- writes for 'The Scotsman' newspaper
- has written a book for children – 'The Perfect Hamburger'
- is international expert on genetics

Alexander Smith was born ....

He went to school and university ....

He lived/worked ....

He wrote/published ....

He has written ....

In his free time ....

He is/has/lives/writes/plays ....

4 Choose one of these detective story writers. Research their life on the Internet or in a library. Make notes, then use your notes to write a short biography.

Agatha Christie (born in Devon)
   Detectives: Miss Marple (British) and Hercule Poirot (Belgian)

Barbara Nadel (born in East London)
   Detectives: Çetin İkmen and Mehmet Suleyman (Turkish)

Raymond Chandler (born in Chicago)
Detective: Philip Marlowe (American)

Lindsey Davis (born in Birmingham)
Detective: Marcus Didio Falco (Ancient Roman)

GRAMMAR

GRAMMAR CHECK

Present Perfect: questions

We make Present Perfect questions with have or has (third person singular) + the past participle.

Where have you been? I was worried.   *Have you seen the fingerprint on the wall?*

We can use the Present Perfect to talk about actions in the recent past, when we don't give an exact time.

1 A news reporter is talking to Inspector Lestrade. Write the reporter's questions using the Present Perfect.

Reporter: a) what / happen / here, Inspector?
............*What has happened here, Inspector?*............

Lestrade: We think that there has been a murder.

Reporter: b) you / find / the body?
....

Lestrade: Yes, we've found some remains in the timber yard.

Reporter: c) you / arrest / anyone yet?
....

Lestrade: Yes, we have. We've arrested a man called John McFarlane.

Reporter: d) where / you / take / him?
....

Lestrade: Scotland Yard. We're talking to him at the moment.

Reporter: e) what / he / tell / you about the crime?
....

Lestrade: Nothing. He's told us a story, but it isn't true.

Reporter: f) Mr Holmes / visit / Deep Dene House?
....

Lestrade: Yes, he has. He knows Mr McFarlane.

Reporter: g) he / help / you with the investigation?
....

Lestrade: No, he hasn't. This is a police investigation.

GRAMMAR CHECK

Present Perfect and Past Simple

We use the Present Perfect for:

- things that happened at an indefinite time in the past (we can use *just* when this time is very recent)

Inspector Lestrade has arrested the criminal.

- experiences in our lives (we can use *never* to mean *at no time*)

I've never done anything bad.   *Holmes has investigated a lot of crimes.*

- things that started in the past and continue up to the present.

I've been here all night.

We use the Past Simple for finished past events.

I took the train to Norwood and arrived there at about nine o'clock.

2 **Complete John McFarlane's note to his mother with the words and verbs in brackets. Use the Present Perfect or Past Simple.**

Dear Mother

I a) .....'ve been..... (be) in this police cell for two days now. I b) ....
(think) a lot about the night when Oldacre c) .... (die), but I don't
understand anything. I d) .... (go) to Deep Dene House on Tuesday night
and Oldacre and I e) .... (talk) for about two hours, but I don't know what
f) .... (happen) later that night. All I know is that I g) ....
(never do) anything wrong in my life.

Lestrade is sure that I h) .... (kill) Oldacre on that night, but that's not
true. I i) .... (meet) him twice in my life. What motive do I have to
kill him? I know that Mr Holmes j) .... (visit) you yesterday. He doesn't
think that I'm guilty but he k) .... (not find) any proof of who is the real
murderer yet. l) I .... (tell) the police everything that I know many times,
but they think that I'm telling lies. And now Lestrade says that they m) ....
(just find) a bloody thumbprint in the house!

You know that I'm innocent, and that helps me a lot. Be strong, Mother.

Your loving son

John

GRAMMAR CHECK

Reflexive pronouns

We use reflexive pronouns (myself, yourself/yourselves, himself, herself, itself, ourselves, themselves) when the object of a sentence is the same person or thing as the subject.

Holmes was asking himself a lot of questions.

We can also use reflexive pronouns to emphasize who did something, or for things that a person does alone without anybody else.

Holmes ate nothing himself.   *I found the fingerprints myself.*

3 **Complete the sentences with reflexive pronouns. Who do you think said each sentence? Write *Holmes, Watson, Lestrade, McFarlane,* or *Mrs Lexington.***

a Don't upset .yourself. , Mrs Lexington.   ....Holmes....

b Mr Oldacre wrote the will .... He asked me to copy it.   ....

c We must ask .... this question, Watson: Why would McFarlane kill him?   ....

d Look at .... in the mirror, Holmes. You look terrible. You slept in that chair last night, didn't you?   ....

e I tried to fight the fire .... , but it was burning so quickly.   ....

f As you can see for .... gentlemen, this is a thumbprint. John McFarlane's thumbprint, in fact.   ....

g Mrs Lexington spoke to McFarlane .... on Tuesday night. She told me that he has evil eyes.   ....

h It was too late to go home, so I found .... a room in a hotel.   ....

i Aren't you eating any breakfast .... , Holmes?   ....

j The thumbprint wasn't there yesterday. I checked the wall ....

k The police have convinced .... that I'm the murderer.   ....

l Do you think that McFarlane put the thumbprint on the wall .... , Watson?   ....

GRAMMAR

GRAMMAR CHECK

Adjective + infinitive

We use be + adjective + infinitive with *to* to express our feelings about something that we or other people do.

I'm sorry to hear this, Mr McFarlane.

Sometimes the adjective describes the infinitive that comes after it, and not the subject of the sentence.

Is it important to know why Oldacre wrote his will on a train?

4 **Complete the interview between Lestrade and McFarlane with the words from the box.**

happy to do	~~surprised to get~~	sorry to say	funny to see
impossible to explain	astonished to read	pleased to meet
easy to understand	happy to leave	sad to learn

Scotland Yard, 23rd August 1894

Investigation: The murder of Mr Jonas Oldacre, 64, of Deep Dene House, Sydenham Road, Norwood

Arrested: Mr John McFarlane, 27, of Torrington Lodge, Blackheath.

Lestrade: How well did you know Jonas Oldacre?

McFarlane: I only met him for the first time two days ago. I knew his name, but I was very
a) *surprised to get* a visit from him on Tuesday in my office.

Lestrade: What did you talk about?

McFarlane: Oldacre said he was b) .... me. He told me that he wanted me to copy a will, and I said that I was c) .... it for him. But when I started to copy the will, I was d) .... that he wanted to leave everything to me! Oldacre laughed, and then said it was e) .... the surprise on my face.

Lestrade: Why do you think that Oldacre wanted to leave you his money?

McFarlane: Well, it isn't very f) .... that. He said that he didn't have any children and that he liked my parents, so he was g) .... the money to me.

Lestrade: Were you h) .... of his death?

McFarlane: Of course I was – and frightened too. You think that I killed him.

Lestrade: Well, perhaps you did. I'm i) .... that we've found your thumbprint in Mr Oldacre's blood. How can you explain that?

McFarlane: I can't. That's j) ...., but I didn't murder him!

GRAMMAR CHECK

Prepositions of time: at, on, in

We use at with times and holidays like *Christmas*. We also say at the weekend, at night, **and** at midnight.

He walked into my office at three o'clock yesterday afternoon.

We use on with days, dates, and expressions with days like *Monday morning* or *Mother's Day*.

The photograph arrived on the day that she married John McFarlane's father.

We use in with weeks, months, seasons, years, and centuries. We also say in the morning, in the afternoon, **and** in the evening.

One morning in the summer of 1894.

5 Complete the sentences with *at*, *on*, or *in*. Then put the sentences in order 1–10.

a Mrs Lexington went to bed ....*at*.... ten thirty and didn't see McFarlane leave. ☐

b Oldacre put a bloody thumbprint on the wall .... Wednesday night. ☐

c The police arrested McFarlane at Sherlock Holmes' house .... about 10 a.m. on Wednesday. ☐

d Early .... Wednesday morning, McFarlane took a train into London after a night in a Norwood hotel. ☐

e Oldacre asked McFarlane to visit him in Norwood .... the evening. ☐

f The crime happened .... August, 1894. ☐ 1

g The police found the thumbprint .... Thursday morning. ☐

h When Sherlock Holmes visited Norwood .... the afternoon on Wednesday, there was no fingerprint on the wall. ☐

i McFarlane arrived at Norwood .... about nine o'clock. ☐

j Oldacre visited McFarlane .... the day of the crime, a Tuesday. ☐

GRAMMAR CHECK

Adjectives ending in –ing and –ed

We use adjectives ending in –ed to talk about how people feel.

I'm interested to hear Mr McFarlane's story.

We use adjectives ending in –ing to talk about the things, events, and people that make us feel different things.

But for me, Watson, life is not so interesting.

6 Choose the correct words to complete the sentences.

a Sherlock Holmes was feeling **boring/bored** because there weren't any crimes to investigate.

b He wanted to investigate an **exciting/excited** murder.

c John McFarlane was very **surprised/surprising** when he read about the murder in the newspaper.

d McFarlane was very **frightening/frightened** when he arrived at Holmes' house because the police were following him.

e Mrs Hudson was **annoyed/annoying** when McFarlane pushed her out of his way.

f Mr Oldacre's will was very **surprised/surprising** because in it he left all his money to John McFarlane.

g Holmes was very **interested/interesting** in the will. He wanted to know why Oldacre wrote it on a train.

h Oldacre was a dangerous man. Mrs McFarlane thought that he was very **frightened/frightening**.

i Lestrade doesn't like answering lots of **annoyed/annoying** questions from Sherlock Holmes when he's investigating a murder.

j Holmes was very **excited/exciting** when he found the bloody thumbprint.

k The thumbprint was an **interested/interesting** problem for Holmes to think about.

l For Watson, living with a man like Holmes is never **boring/bored**.

GRAMMAR CHECK

Adjectives ending in –y and adverbs ending in –ly

We use adjectives to describe people or things. They go before nouns, or after verbs of appearance, like *be, seem*, and *look*. Some adjectives end in –y.

Please don't be angry, Mr Holmes.

We often use adverbs to describe how something happens. Most adverbs of this type end in –ly.

Holmes walked slowly to the front door.

Some adjectives, such as *brotherly, fatherly, friendly*, and *motherly*, end in –ly too.

7 Complete the sentences with the correct adjectives and adverbs from the box. Write adjective or adverb after the word.

> dry   carefully   hungry   daily   happy   angry   ~~deeply~~   sunny   weekly   quickly
>
> angrily   thoughtfully   ~~early~~   friendly   happily   warmly   busy

a Watson went to bed *early (adjective)*, but Holmes didn't want to sleep. He was playing the violin and thinking *deeply (adverb)* about the investigation.

b Holmes was looking at the letter very .... 'I'm not sure what happened here,' he said .... , 'but I will find the answer.'

c I thanked Mr Oldacre .... for leaving me the money in his will. I thought that he was a very .... person.

d The wood was very .... after the warm weather, and it burned very

....

e Oldacre was very .... when John's mother married another man.

f It was a beautiful, ... afternoon, but Holmes wasn't feeling

....

g Watson was reading the .... newspaper when Holmes came in. He was smiling .... 'I've found the answer in today's *Times*!' he said.

h 'Aren't you .... , Holmes? You haven't eaten anything.'

i It was Friday. Lestrade was writing his .... report when Sergeant Judd knocked on his door. 'Come back later!' he said, ... 'Can't you see that I'm .... ?'

DOMINOES Your Choice

Read *Dominoes* for pleasure, or to develop language skills. It's your choice.

Each *Domino* reader includes:
- a good story to enjoy
- integrated activities to develop reading skills and increase vocabulary
- task-based projects – perfect for CEFR portfolios
- contextualized grammar activities

Each *Domino* pack contains a reader, and an excitingly dramatized audio recording of the story

If you liked this *Domino*, read these:

The Three Musketeers
Alexandre Dumas

It is the year 1627, and young d'Artagnan comes to Paris with a dream – to become a King's Musketeer. Three of these brave soldiers – Porthos, Athos and Aramis – soon become his friends. After a short time d'Artagnan has fallen in love – and into great danger. Can the three musketeers and d'Artagnan fight against the evil plans of the beautiful Milady and the cruel Cardinal Richelieu?

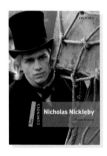

Nicholas Nickleby
Charles Dickens

When his father dies a poor man, Nicholas Nickleby goes to London with his mother and sister, Kate. He hopes for help from his rich Uncle Ralph. But Ralph Nickleby is only interested in making money.

So Nicholas takes a teaching job at Dotheboys Hall – a terrible school belonging to Mr Wackford Squeers. There he helps a poor boy called Smike who has no one to look after him.

Leaving Dotheboys, Nicholas makes both friends and enemies on his journey towards better things. But will Smike, who travels with him, ever find the happy family life that he so dearly wants?

	CEFR	Cambridge Exams	IELTS	TOEFL iBT	TOEIC
Level 3	B1	PET	4.0	57-86	550
Level 2	A2–B1	KET-PET	3.0-4.0	–	390
Level 1	A1–A2	YLE Flyers/KET	3.0	–	225
Starter & Quick Starter	A1	YLE Movers	1.0–2.0	–	–

You can find details and a full list of books and teachers' resources on our website:
www.oup.com/elt/gradedreaders